Mourning Into Dancing:

Saying Goodbye to Grief

Stan E. DeKoven, Ph.D.

Mourning Into Dancing

Saying Goodbye to Grief

Stan E. DeKoven, Ph.D.

Copyright 2014 © Stan E. DeKoven

ISBN # 978-1-61529-147-2

Vision Publishing
1672 Main St., E109
Ramona, California 92065
www.booksbyvision.com

Printed in the United States of America

Adapted from Grief Relief and other resources

No part of this book may be reproduced in any form, without the express, written permission of the author.

Table of Contents

Foreword 7

Acknowledgments 9

Chapter One: There is Hope 11

Chapter Two: Understanding the Mystery 17

Chapter Three: The Word Works 33

Chapter Four: Say Goodbye; Say Hello 39

Chapter Five: Grief Relief 45

Chapter Six: Joy Comes in the Mourning 55

A Typical Testimony

"Last July 28, my husband of 34 years unexpectedly passed away. Although Stan had some physical problems during the last 4 years, he always had good medical checkups. His problems were with his frame and mobility due to extreme arthritis and constant pain. So, when he drew his last breath sitting next to me watching the NASCAR race, my world turned upside down.

Having the opportunity to read this book was painful, comforting, informative, and inspirational. Throughout the reading process I felt that Dr. Stan was talking directly to me; page after page, so many of the explanations and examples resonated with me. It was difficult to keep reading sometimes, but in the end having the opportunity to read this survival manual was a blessing.

I praise the Lord for providing me with the "prescription" I needed, and I thank you and Dr. Stan for the opportunity to receive it. I am certain this book can and will help many who are attempting to survive a devastating loss."

Sincerely,

Maria Shrider
Findlay, Ohio

Recommendation

"Dear Stan,

Thanks again for giving me the opportunity to read your book. As I mentioned, when I first received and read it I was in a fog. Though there was great information, I really wasn't thinking clearly enough to say anything about it, well almost anything. Just reading the book was a blessing.

One thing that I thought would be helpful was some sort of a pull-out page that would be a quick reference to remind readers of the points made in the book. As I read the book, I found it helpful to know I am not crazy, or overthinking my emotions, but indeed I experienced many of the emotions that are part of the grieving process. It would also help me to look at the ways I can pick myself up and make the right choices to get through the day. Reading a "reference list" would be easier than trying to find the information in the book. ...."

Susan Slusher, Director
Christian International Equipping Network
Santa Rosa Beach, FL

For more information and to get your free copy of the reference guide, go to www.drstandekoven.com .

6

Foreword

I wish I did not have as much experience with loss, grief and mourning as I do, but I do. I have buried two wives, my mom, and a few other significant relatives and friends. In addition I have walked with many men and women through the painful journey of loss and grief. Every man and woman will meet grief many times along the path of life, for it is truly a part of life.

We mourn for lost loved ones; we "feel bad" (a form of mourning) when we move away from old friends; we "hurt" when we lose an important job; we feel "devastated" in a divorce. Of course, the greatest grief is usually experienced when we lose a spouse or, God forbid, a child.

As a practicing family counselor, former pastor, and current teacher of practical theology, I have helped hundreds of precious people work through the grief process. However, in this booklet we will discover grief and mourning have some common characteristics which no two people experience in the same way. Grief and mourning are a journey; it is a journey best walked with someone possessing knowledge of the journey, a listening ear, and an open heart.

This booklet is written as a companion for the sufferer. It is not a substitute for a good counselor, strong and loving family, pastor, etc. But it will help cut to the chase in regards to what to expect as you begin a journey no one wants to walk. This book has been specifically written to help the counselor, pastor, lay-leader minister, and the hurting person to:

- 1. Recognize the grief relief process,
- 2. Accept it as normal, and then
- 3. Learn how to work through the mourning process, utilizing the transforming and sustaining power of Jesus Christ as found in the word of God and practical wisdom.

I pray that the tools of ministry which God has given me in my counseling practice will help each person reading this book to learn how to reduce the trauma of loss in their life, and increase the joy of their Christ-centered walk.

Dr. Stan

Acknowledgments

I deeply appreciate the Church of Jesus Christ -- it is alive, vibrant, and powerfully able to give care and comfort to those in need.

Further, I am grateful to the Lord for his power to reconcile and restore all who have suffered the loss of a loved one. To you, I say, "His grace is sufficient!"

Dedication

This book is dedicated especially dedicated to key people in my life: Karen S. DeKoven, Carma Louise DeKoven, Jack Frates, Shirley Frates, Noreen DeKoven Shehadi, Dr. Joe Bohac, Dr. Doug Jarrard, Dr. Anthony Spero and Rev. David Jones. You are loved and missed; we honor you.

10

Chapter One:

There is Hope

In Proverbs 13:12 it states;

"Hope deferred makes the heart sick."

Whether one experiences a loss suddenly or over a prolonged period of time, a loss affects our hope -- hope that we would have another vacation, hope we would see grandkids together, hope that I would finally get the job I wanted. Hope deferred, certainly makes one sad, but life does not have to be hopeless, even when we have suffered a major loss. We always have hope.

There are all types of losses...and there is hope regardless of the type or intensity of the loss. These losses may include: the loss of relationships in general, more specifically the loss of a friend, separation of husband and wives, loss of children, divorce, separation from animals, loss of a job or status, etc.

"You have turned for me my mourning into dancing; You have loosed my sackcloth and girded me with gladness." Psalms 30:11

Regardless of the loss, grief and mourning are the natural reactions to the loss, but in time we can experience life again; it requires process, grace, faith and time.

Mourning in American Culture

Part of the average person's difficulty with grief and grieving is that our American culture no longer validates our status as a griever. There are few helps or symbols (such as a black armband) to acknowledge that you are grieving beyond the funeral. Society has taught us that overt displays of grief are not acceptable past a week or two after loss. Many men and women who have lost a loved one later complain that there is subtle (and sometimes not so subtle) pressure placed upon them to get over the loss, to "behave normally" as if nothing has changed in their lives.

People continue to receive messages from their family, friends and employers to "get a grip," "get on with life," and "it's time to get over this" as soon as two or three weeks after a death of a loved one. Americans haven't learned that people suffer deeply, emotionally, and sometimes physically, even though they may not be showing overt symptoms of grief.

Most other cultures are far more realistic about how long mourning requires. Many have the custom of dressing in black for up to six months or a year. It is the Orthodox

Jewish custom to offer formal prayers daily for 11 Hebrew months and to mourn for 12 months.

If you would like to give your family, friends, and employers something that explains your grieving behavior, consider using this letter.

My Dear (Family, Friends, Pastor, Employer...)

As you know I have recently experienced the death/loss of my (   ).

This loss is devastating to me, and it will take time for me to work through my grief. Sometimes I fear that you may expect me to heal quickly, but grief cannot be rushed.

I will cry more often than usual for a while. My tears symbolize the release of my feelings and are a healthy sign that I am recovering. These tears are neither a sign of personal weakness nor a lack of faith or hope.

Because my emotions are heightened by the strain of grief, I may seem irrational at times. Please be patient and forgiving, if I become irritable and angry for no apparent reason. Grief comes in unpredictable ways and sometimes at inconvenient moments.

I know that you are probably at a loss for what to do or say to help me. There are no magic words you can say to take my pain away. Touch me or give me a hug to let me know you care.

Please don't wait for me to call you. I am often too overwhelmed to think of reaching out for help. I need you more than ever in the months ahead, but my pride sometimes prevents me from telling you. Give me space to heal, but don't allow me to withdraw from you.

Pray for me, if you wish; but pray that I will find the courage and the strength I need to deal with my grief constructively. Faith is necessary in every area of life, and the process of grief is no exception.

If by chance you have had a similar loss, please share it with me. It will not make me feel worse. Grief shared is grief diminished.

Telling me to "cheer up, it could be worse" makes me feel discounted and angry. This loss is the worst thing for me right now. But I will heal and live again. While there are still painful days ahead for me, I will not always feel as intensely as I do now. One day I will be able to laugh again and find new joy in living.

I appreciate your concern and caring. Your understanding and support is a gift, which I will always treasure.

Sincerely,

I have told many fellow mourners that grief can be a gift, especially when someone tries to be too nosey, too helpful, too...well you know, and telling them to leave you well enough alone can always be excused, because we are grieving -- use it as necessary!

For His anger is but for a moment, His favor is for a lifetime; Weeping may last for the night, But a shout of joy comes in the morning. Psalms 30:5

16

Chapter Two:

Understanding the Mystery

A friend told me, shortly after my bride Karen had died, that Jesus needed another angel in heaven, and that is why the Lord took Karen. Nonsense. God is not cruel, and no doubt, he has plenty of angels. I know the person was trying to comfort me, but really, I just wanted to smack him. Ignoring ignorance is a skill you will probably have to learn as you grieve.

Not one of us is immune to grief. Grief comes to everyone, and it comes in many different ways. No matter how you experience the pain of loss -- the grief cycle triggers a myriad of emotions. Everyone processes through grief differently; don't let anyone try to steal away your personal journey.

Because grief is unique, each of us responds to it in varying ways. Much of our response to grief is based on our incorporated belief system, that is -- how our parents, church and other social/cultural influences have taught us to respond. However, there are some common traits, which we can draw upon to help us understand most of the common attributes of grief. But first, some common myths:

Common Myths about Grief

- All losses are the same.
- All bereaved people grieve in the same way.
- It takes two weeks to three months to get over your grief.
- When grief is resolved, it never comes up again.
- It is better to put painful thoughts out of your mind.
- Anger should not be a part of your grief.
- Children need to be protected from grief and death.
- You will have no relationship with your loved one after death or divorce.
- The intensity and length of your grief are a testimony to your love for the deceased.
- Only sick people have physical problems in their grief.
- Funerals and rituals are unimportant in helping us heal.
- It is best to stay in control and keep a "stiff upper lip."
- It is best to put the memories of your loved one in the past and go on with your life.
- It is best to get involved and stay busy.
- Crying doesn't solve anything.

Making changes can be difficult as we are impacted by the beliefs and feelings of those around us. Don't believe the myths presented above; they are neither true nor helpful. It is not easy to change traditions and long held beliefs or expectations. But, when it is in our best interest, we can learn new habits and make necessary changes. Some of the common experiences related to grief and mourning are described in the following paragraphs.

Grief Is Painful

The initial response to grief is simple -- it hurts! You may feel tightness in your stomach or in your throat. You may experience persistent headaches or nausea. You may notice dryness in your mouth. Your body may not move as you want it to. You may feel shortness of breath as if you need to breathe deeply or to sigh.

King David experienced intense grief at the loss of his son. As with most fathers, his son was the love of his life, and the grief that he experienced is a feeling common to all of us. God's Word details for us both David's loss of a child and his reaction to it. (2 Samuel 12:1-25)

Physical responses to loss are a normal part of the initial grief reaction.

Grief Is Directional

Healthy grief moves naturally through several stages to a point of accepting your loss. In time, you begin to feel and act like your former self. If you are feeling intense pangs of grief right now, the important thing to know is that your pain may be the best indication that you are moving through a healthy, natural process of mourning and grieving.

Grief Is Personal

No one feels grief exactly as you feel it! Your feelings and your circumstances are unique. You must not fall into the trap of thinking you are alone and isolate yourself from others. Although they may not be openly grieving now, most of your friends have experienced some sort of grief, and they can help you. Let them help! Withdrawing from those who love you will only intensify the pain you feel and prolong the healing process.

Grief Moves Slowly

When a loved one dies, or when you experience any other significant loss, pretending as if nothing has happened prolongs the process. Your loss is difficult and significant, because it is personal; it happened to you.

It is natural that almost everything else may seem suddenly unimportant, such as your job, other family members, and daily tasks. You may be anxious to overcome this feeling of meaninglessness. However, it is important to recognize that this lack of interest in other things is thoroughly normal, and it won't last.

Grief moves slowly, and in time personal meaning in life will return -- also slowly. You must not condemn yourself for not meeting some imaginary timetable for your mourning. There is no time table, but there are some guidelines. [1]

A close friend of mine had spent nearly five years in full-time ministry when a public agency said he couldn't do his work any longer. His loss was so powerful that he lay on the couch for nearly three months depressed and in despair -- so many of his hopes and dreams seemed shattered. He felt abandoned, alone, and lost.

But with time, he was restored. His former ministry was but a mere shadow of his present work.

Grief Includes Mixed Feelings

Websters New World Dictionary. Warren Books. 1987. defines grief as "an intense emotional suffering caused by a loss."

The feelings associated with grief may be physical, emotional, even spiritual, and they are very real. Do not hide from the feelings, but learn to express them in healthy ways.

The grief experience may also include feelings of guilt and hostility, which are sometimes not accepted as "normal" in our Christian culture (as Christians, many say we should

---

[1] See page 45 for **Fifteen Tips to Expedite The Mourning to Dancing Process.**

"rejoice" that our loved one has gone to be with the Lord -- without ever allowing time to mourn the physical separation).

Guilt, Hostility, and Anger

Almost every grieving person feels some guilt and anger, and it is often directed at God!

Perhaps you have asked, "Why did this happen to me?" So does almost everyone else.

A young woman's husband has died. She is now required to make several major adjustments rather rapidly. She suddenly becomes both mother and father to her children. She must find work, and she may be forced to sell the home in which she has lived for most of her married life. She will need to make many other radical adjustments, because there is usually insufficient money to handle these major changes.

These sudden and frequently drastic demands may cause the young lady to become angry. This anger is both normal and understandable. The best thing she can do is to express this anger openly to a trusted friend or to a competent counselor.

Hiding or repressing anger only makes it worse, and it will surface at some other time in life -- usually against someone who does not deserve to be on the receiving end of the angry outburst.

During the grieving process it is natural for a person to feel anger directed toward the deceased, toward God, toward the boss who fired them from a job or toward the world in general. This is a transitory response to the tremendous and significant loss suffered. To the grieving person, death or any other loss experienced always seems unfair.

Remember, it is natural for your most frequent questions to be "Why?" "Why did God do this to me?" "Why is life so unfair?" These questions really mean, "I am angry because this terrible event happened to me." This is a normal response. Only when it becomes unresolved, dragging on for prolonged periods, will it give bitterness an opportunity to develop. The Bible wisely warns of the dangers of unresolved anger:

> *"In your anger do not sin: Do not let the sun go down while you are still angry, and do not give the devil a foothold" (Ephesians 4:26-27, NIV).*

It is acceptable to express anger, but only if it is controlled, and is of a short duration.

Forgiveness, and letting go of hostility, are necessary to resolve your grief. You need to forgive your former spouse who divorced you. Forgive your former boss who fired you. Forgive your deceased spouse for leaving you (remember, this is emotional, not always rational). Then move on with your life. Of course, forgiveness is not an event, but a process, and is required for healthy growth.

Grief Is Natural and Healthy

Grief is a natural and healthy response to a significant personal loss. As you try to think about grief as natural and healthy, consider these following situations. They are all part of the normal grief process. There are several normal reactions that a person may experience. Some reactions are explained in the following paragraphs.

"I Can't Talk"

You may find it extremely difficult to talk about your deceased loved one or other significant loss. For a period of time, you may say to others, "I'm sorry, I just do not want to talk about it." This is perfectly all right. Do not permit your friends to force you into discussing your loss before you feel ready. Eventfully you will want to talk.

One grieving woman I knew was very close to her older sister. When that older sister died of cancer, the younger woman avoided all conversations about the deceased sister. She constantly changed the subject when it related to her older sister. She simply did not want to deal with the loss, and so she strenuously avoided any talk of the matter for several weeks.

Obsessive Reactions

You may find yourself eating, even when your food tastes bland and uninteresting. Under severe stress, we tend to regress toward behaviors that give us a quick sense of comfort. One of these "regressive" behaviors is eating comfort foods that are not all that healthy for us.

There may be other comfort behaviors that you may regress towards such as sleeping in a fetal position, avoiding strangers, etc. Don't fear them, they are usually temporary.

Out of Touch

You may look at a letter from a friend without reading it, almost as if neither you, nor the letter are really there. A friend may be talking to you for ten minutes and you may not hear a word. You might be driving to an appointment and drive right past the place where you were supposed to go. All of these reactions are normal, due to a temporary lack of concentration. In time, this too will disappear.

Talking Out Loud

You may find yourself talking out loud to your lost loved one as though he or she were still present. You may catch yourself criticizing your ex-spouse out loud in an empty room for "something else" you just thought about that makes you angry. You are not really crazy; you are grieving. Try and relax, as this is simply a part of the process.

Memories

You may feel stabbing grief when you see a reminder of your loved one, such as a photograph, a stamp collection, or a best friend. Such reactions may occur even after you thought you had accepted your loss and returned to normal.

In divorce, old places trigger old memories -- especially old friends whom you unexpectedly meet at the market or church. Many people who experience divorce find it necessary to make a whole new set of friends to escape the constant reminders of the departed spouse. Divorce is like death, but in some ways worse, as the "corpse" is still walking around!

Reactions

You may laugh out loud in a room when you think about funny memories involving you and the person who has died. At the same time, you may feel guilt for laughing irreverently.

Forget the guilt. This is a normal reaction. Laughter often occurs at funerals -- where a person laughs almost without control. This is often misinterpreted as a lack of respect. IT IS NOT! It is simply one way that the nervous system tries to cope with the stress of loss. Humor often helps us experience GRIEF RELIEF during the difficult days of adjustment after the loss of a job, a death, or any other significant loss.

Withdrawal

You may want to withdraw from those around you. Withdrawal, like denial, takes many forms. You may withdraw from the pain of grief by turning to alcohol or other drugs.

You may try to escape grief by over activity, such as throwing yourself into your work, or joining clubs or groups, over-committing your time so you do not have to feel the pain of grief.
You may even temporarily contemplate suicide, the ultimate attempt to withdraw. In these times, always call on Christ for strength, **and** seek counseling.

If withdrawing is keeping you from the normal functions of life, you need to seek professional help. There are people who care and can help you. God cares about you, and he has others prepared to assist you through your mourning process.

Self-pity

You may experience self-pity. Grief hurts; give attention to your pain. You are expected to take care of your emotional wounds. However, self-pity becomes a problem when, months after the death, or other significant loss, your consistent conversation starter is something like this: "No one knows how hard life is for me."

The person mired in self-pity proceeds to recite a list of all the bad things that have happened to them. This process is futile; instead of helping, it only serves to perpetuate the pain. Perhaps a reminder from Paul the apostle will help:

> *Finally, brethren, whatever is true, whatever is honorable, whatever is right, whatever is pure, whatever is lovely, whatever is of good repute, if there is any excellence and if anything worthy of praise, let your mind dwell on these things (Philippians 4:8 NASB).*

What a powerful bit of advice that, when applied over time, can produce significant comfort, even joy.

Self-pity is often used to get attention. Self-pity blinds you to the good things in life, both past and present. It is best to seek positive ways to get the attention needed, such as saying to a friend, "I need a hug," or to occupy your time by inviting a friend for dinner or out to a movie.

These eight varied reactions are not all inclusive -- you may experience other reactions. Are they normal? Yes! Are they healthy? Yes, if they occur within reasonable timeframes.

Guilt – A Useless Emotion

During your period of grieving, you may likely experience some guilt. Guilt is a problem when it controls or dominates you, or when it blinds you to the possibility of resolving your grief and returning to normal living.

A mother reluctantly gave her son permission to buy a motorcycle, knowing that if she did not grant the permission, the son would have found a way to get the motorcycle anyway. About six months after the boy started riding the bike, he was in a fatal accident. When the woman entered counseling, she had spent nearly four years mourning the loss of her son -- and blaming herself for the accident (after all, she gave him permission to buy the motorcycle).

Her guilt became her obsession, and everything else in life was neglected. The consequences of her guilt included her husband divorcing her, and her friends stopped visiting her. She became a hermit, ruining her life – the guilt over the death of a son was more than useless, it became destructive -- her son was gone, and nothing she could do would change that.

Remember, Jesus really does love us, and freely pardons any transgression. If Jesus can forgive us, then we need to receive his forgiveness as well. He is there for us during the "valley" of our "shadow."

Because of all the cross of Jesus provides, we can be set free from irrational guilt. To be free from useless guilt, take the following steps:

Step One

Acknowledge your need for forgiveness, either of your "sin," or your partner's, or others, and then forgive.

Step Two

Forgive yourself, but first express the negative feelings about yourself that have been causing the guilt, and then forgive yourself for these transgressions.

Step Three

Accept the Lord's forgiveness according to the Word of God.

"If we confess our sins, he is faithful and just to forgive us our sins, and to cleanse us from all unrighteousness" (I John 1:9).

Step Four

Resist the thoughts, which can come from Satan or your own mind, which condemn you in any way. Romans 8:1 and James 4:7 are helpful.

"There is therefore no condemnation to those in Christ" and

"Submit yourselves therefore to God. Resist the devil, and he will flee from you" (James 4:7).

Step Five

You must cast down (confess, talk about, throw down) vain (useless) imaginations or thought patterns. In II Corinthians 10: 4-5 we find,

"For the weapons of our warfare are not fleshly, but mighty through God to the destruction of fortresses; Casting down imaginations, and every high thing that exalts itself above the knowledge of God, and bring captive every thought to the obedience of Christ."

When you morbidly dwell on your "worthlessness," you must cast down those thoughts and embrace what God says about you. Thoughts such as, "you are loved by God" (John 3:16); "You are fearfully and wonderfully made (Psalm 139:14); you are a new creation in Christ (II Corinthians 5:17); are the kinds of thoughts you should focus upon.

Grief Often Brings Denial

Some forms of denial over the death of a loved one, the break-up of a marriage, or even the loss of a job, are natural. This is particularly true in the early stages of grief. Denial becomes a problem only when it is prolonged or extreme.

Denial of death for months and years after the departure of a loved one usually means that the bereaved person is also denying other important aspects of life, such as personal appearance or healthy relationships with others.
If this is a problem, talk it over with someone you can trust, someone who will be honest with you. Your pastor or good Christian counselors are the kind of people who can help.

Most professionals now believe that normal grief can last as long as 1 year for every 5 years of marriage. For some, adjustment may not mean remarriage or finding a job like the previous one, or replacing your dog. Everyone handles it differently.

Chapter Three:

The Word Works

"Precious in the eyes of the Lord are the death of his saints" (Psalm 116:15)

Many well-meaning, but ill informed, pastors and lay leaders have taught that if we are true Christians, grief and subsequent mourning of loss should not be experienced. Since Christians are triumphant over death, and since heaven is assured, we should rejoice over the loss of a believing spouse, friend, or child. Unfortunately, these individuals have missed the whole council of God. Grief is a biblical concept. We see it throughout the Bible, as we will discover here.

Old Testament Pictures

In the Old Testament, nine different words are translated as "grief" from the original Hebrew. They are as follows:

- *Morah*, which is translated to mean bitterness or trouble (Genesis 26:35),
- *Kaac*, meaning vexation, anger, angry indignation, provocation, sore, sorrow, spite, wrath (Job 6:12; I Samuel 1:16; Psalm 6:7; 31:9).

- ***Puwgah***, is translated to mean a stumbling block.
- ***Makob***, is translated as anguish, affliction, pain and sorrow (2 Chron. 6:29; Psalm 69:26),
- ***Kaeb***, is translated as suffering adversity both mental and physical (John 2:13; 16:3).
- ***Yagown***, translates to affliction and sorrow (Psalm 31:10; Jeremiah 45:3).
- ***Chalah***, which stands for a primitive root to be rubbed or worn, or figuratively to be weak, sick, afflicted, to grieve, to make sick, also to stroke or flattering (Isaiah 17:11; 53:10),
- ***Choliy***, meaning malady, anxiety, calamity, disease (Isaiah 53:3; Jeremiah 6:7,10-19).
- ***Yagah***, has the meaning to grieve, sorrow or vex (Lam. 3:32).

Job suffered great grief as did Jacob over his loss of Joseph, as did David over the loss of his baby. In Isaiah chapter 53 we see that grief was a characteristic that would be seen in the life of the Messiah. The experience of grief varied from sorrow to anxiety, illness, affliction, adversity, anguish, bitterness, anger, indignation, trouble, and it was experienced as a stumbling block to enjoying life.

New Testament

The Greek words for grief and sorrow include *lupeo*, which means to distress, to be sad or to cause grief (2 Corinthians 2:5). The expression of grief is found in the word *stenazo*, which is to sigh, to murmur, pray audibly with grief, groans and grudge (Hebrews 13:17). The word *lupe*, which is translated sadness, grief, heaviness and sorrow (I Peter 2:19). Paul and Peter both described (and no doubt experienced) grief. However, none of the New Testament characters experienced grief from loss like Jesus did. At the grave of Lazarus, in the garden of Gethsemane, and certainly on the cross, Jesus experienced intense grief; however, he was in every way the consummate overcomer.

Mourning

The process of grief is often called mourning. There are several Old and New Testament words translated as mourning. It was Jesus who taught on the mountain, *"Blessed are those who mourn, for they shall be comforted (Mat 5:4 NASB).*

What happens to those who never mourn?

Let us examine these important words regarding mourning. The first word found in the Hebrew is **caphad**, which means to tear the hair and beat the breast, also to lament, akin to that word is **nuwd**, meaning to console, to bemoan, flee and to be sorrowful. Further, we have **gadar**, which means to mourn or to cause to mourn, **naham**, to growl, mourn or roar, **ebel**, to lament, or mourn, **abal and abel**, to bewail, lament and mourn.

In the Hebrew tradition, mourning was not done in isolation but was open, loud, and filled with robust emotional expression.

In the New Testament there are two words, ***pentheo*** and ***kopto***, meaning to grieve, to beat the breast, cut down and to mourn.

In both the Old and New Testaments, in the lives of both saints and sinners, the downcast and the divine, a common unavoidable response to loss was (and is today) grief and mourning. Though there may be no escaping the impact of loss, there is hope as we understand that God is with us as we process through with God's help.

Unfortunately for many, the lack of healthy grieving leaves one depressed, having never experienced the comfort of The Holy Spirit, who is readily available for us.

> *Jesus wept. So the Jews were saying, "See how He love him!" (John 11:35-36)*

> *Cast your burden upon the LORD, and He will sustain you; He will never allow the righteous to be shaken (Psalms 55:22 NASB).*

> *For all things are for your sakes, so that the grace which is spreading to more and more people may cause the giving of thanks to abound to the glory of God.*

> *Therefore we do not lose heart, but though our outer man is decaying, yet our inner man is being renewed day by day (2 Corinthians 4:15-16 NASB).*

The LORD is near to the brokenhearted, And saves those who are crushed in spirit. (Psalms 34:18 NASB).

Blessed be the God and Father of our Lord Jesus Christ, who according to His great mercy has caused us to be born again to a living hope through the resurrection of Jesus Christ from the dead, [4] to obtain an inheritance which is imperishable and undefiled and will not fade away, reserved in heaven for you, [5] who are protected by the power of God through faith for a salvation ready to be revealed in the last time. (1 Peter1:3-5 NASB)

Chapter Four:

Say Goodbye; Say Hello

Death is as much a mystery as it is painful and real. Death and other significant losses leave us with a feeling of bewilderment and frustration.

As you grieve, you feel the mystery. You ask "Why?" and no one seems to have an adequate answer.

You hurt, and no one seems able to erase the pain.

But through the power of Jesus Christ, we can put death, or any loss, in the context of our Christian faith and hope.

> *And after you have suffered for a little while, the God of all grace, who called you to His eternal glory in Christ, will Himself perfect, confirm, strengthen and establish you.*
>
> *To Him be dominion forever and ever. Amen. (1 Peter 5:10-11 NASB)*

Do you see it? Your Christian walk affirms death, loss, and grief as a natural part of life. The Christian faith sees death in two parts:

   1. As the cessation of physical life, or

2. As alienation from God.

To a Christian, the only death that matters in the eternal framework of things is when we are alienated from God.

The threat of death, with both of its meanings, is the oasis for God's action in providing the means to salvation. Salvation through Jesus Christ is offered to save us from sin and death. As paradoxical as it seems, if there were no death, there would be no hope.

> *"He who has found his life shall lose it, and he who has lost his life for My sake shall find it. (Matthew 10:39 NASB)*

The fact that death and grief are a part of the Christian life sets us free to accept loss by death, or any other loss, as natural and inevitable. Questions like, "Why did God let him die?" or "Why were my hopes lost?" take on new meaning. When you understand death from a Christian perspective, then anger at God, though being a somewhat normal response, is not a necessary one.

Loss is a natural part of life. Blame is not necessary when we accept a Christian view of death and dying.

> *We know that we have passed out of death into life, because we love the brethren. He who does not love abides in death (1 John 3:14 NASB).*

Christian fellowship is an affirmation of life. The Christian fellowship, through your local church, should demonstrate life out of death. During your grief relief period, your church community will hopefully say to you, "We stand with you and believe that God is the source of life. We comfort you in your grief.

Do you see the great significance in Christian fellowship? This is seen in a simple truth from the Bible:

> *"And they continued in the apostles' doctrine and fellowship, and in breaking of bread, and in prayers" (Acts 2:42).*

You must not feel that you are a burden to your church community. You actually rob them of a blessing by refusing to accept their sincere help.

> *The one who does not love does not know God, for God is love (1 John 4:8 NASB).*

Your hope is found in your relationship with God. He is the source of your hope. God loves you. Even Jesus, when he faced death on the cross, cried,

> *And about the ninth hour Jesus cried out with a loud voice, saying, "ELI, ELI, LAMA SABACHTHANI?" that is, "MY GOD, MY GOD, WHY HAST THOU FORSAKEN ME?" (Matthew 27:46 NASB).*

Yet, a short time later,

> *And Jesus, crying out with a loud voice, said, "Father, INTO THY HANDS I COMMIT MY SPIRIT." And having said this, He breathed His last (Luke 23:46 NASB).*

When you yield to God, this victorious step guarantees that there is hope in the face of death and grief. Hope, death, and grief are natural. Hope remains after death, and grief is gone.

> *But we do not want you to be uninformed, brethren, about those who are asleep, that you may not grieve, as do the rest who have no hope (1 Thessalonians 4:13 NASB).*

Neither death nor grief can separate us from God's love.

> *Who shall separate us from the love of Christ? Shall tribulation, or distress, or persecution, or famine, or nakedness, or peril, or sword?*

> *Just as it is written,*
> *"FOR THY SAKE WE ARE BEING PUT TO DEATH ALL DAY LONG; WE WERE CONSIDERED AS SHEEP TO BE SLAUGHTERED."*

> *But in all these things we overwhelmingly conquer through Him who loved us.*

For I am convinced that neither death, nor life, nor angels, nor principalities, nor things present, nor things to come, nor powers, nor height, nor depth, nor any other created thing, shall be able to separate us from the love of God, which is in Christ Jesus our Lord (Romans 8:35-39 NASB.

Let me summarize some of the steps you can take to work through grief:

1. Don't ignore your feelings.
    Tears are normal, natural, and essential. Allow yourself the privilege of talking or crying. Give yourself permission to feel.

2. Do not punish yourself.
    Often we blame ourselves for real or imaginary wrongs which can keep us from being productive. We know that our Lord loves us unconditionally. Thus, we must work toward full acceptance of our loss and not hold ourselves responsible for what we cannot change.

3. You are not alone.
    Though your loss is yours, you are not the only one who has experienced loss.

4. Take time.
   Healing takes time. For major losses, it often takes up to two years to process through heavy grief. You must tend to your emotional trauma as you would a physical wound. Thus, postpone major decisions in your life until your healing is well on its way.

The ultimate goal of this process is to find peace of mind. This does not happen through a simple prayer, trite phrases, or "just getting on with life." The longer and more intimate the relationship -- the longer the time to heal. Trust God in the process.

Chapter Five:

Grief Relief

Fifteen Tips to Expedite The Mourning to Dancing Process

Here are fifteen key ideas to keep in your mind when you are dealing with grief resulting from death or any significant loss.

1. Nurture Your Relationship With God

If you have been inactive in your relationship with God, there could never be a better time to become involved again with spiritual matters. The Bible is of great comfort and it has much to say about the nature of sorrow.

> *The righteous cry and the LORD hears, And delivers them out of all their troubles.*
>
> *The LORD is near to the brokenhearted, And saves those who are crushed in spirit.*
>
> *Many are the afflictions of the righteous; But the LORD delivers him out of them all. (Psalms 34:17-19 NASB)*

If you already have a strong relationship with God, you may experience a temporary distancing from Him during this time of grief.

As time passes, you will find most people who are initially angry at God will release their anger and become close to Him again.

2. Accept the Grief

As I shared earlier in this booklet, during a significant loss is not the time to "try and be brave." Take the time to cry.

It is all right to hurt, and it is a necessary and natural process. Do not condemn yourself, or accept the condemnation of others because you are not "trusting in God" or are "lacking in faith." God has designed you to release your natural pain through real tears.

3. Talk About Your Loss

Share your grief with your family; do not attempt to protect each other by awkward silences. Find a friend to talk to, or anyone else who will listen to your hurts without passing judgment.

If possible, find someone who has experienced a similar sorrow and can share some common experiences with you.

4. Keep Busy

This sounds like avoidance, but it is not. I am suggesting that you find purposeful work that occupies your mind.

When I suggest you "stay busy," I am not suggesting you buzz around in frantic, mindless activity. But when a "part of you" has died through loss of a loved one or another grief situation, it is vital that the "part of you" that is left, be somehow productive. Some suggestions:

- Work as a volunteer at church
- Serve in your community.
- Become a reader to children.

In short, pick healthy, worthwhile, activities centered upon others to occupy your time and keep your mind from meditating excessively on your own hurts. By meeting the needs of others, you will find yourself simultaneously meeting your own needs.

5. Take Care Of Yourself

Bereavement can be a threat to your health. At the moment, you may feel that "you don't care" about your body or your health. It is vital for you to realize that your needs are important.

Your life is valuable; care for it. Jesus valued you enough to give His life for you.

> *"But God demonstrates his own love for us in this: While we were still sinners, Christ died for us"*
> *(Romans 5:8 NIV)*

You see, he loves you and sees you as infinitely important to him.

6. Eat Well

At this time of emotional and physical depletion, your body needs good nourishment more than at any other time. Many people do not feel like cooking and turn to fast-food restaurants for quick meals. Fast-foods are typically high in fat, salt, and calories. Therefore it is unhealthy for long term health.

Loss of appetite may also be a problem. If you can only pick at your food, a vitamin supplement might be helpful, but it will not make up fully for a poor diet. If you sense your body is growing weaker and weaker, you may need to see your family doctor to ensure that your health is maintained.

7. Exercise Regularly

Return to your old exercise program, or start one as soon as possible. Depression can be reduced somewhat by the biochemical changes brought about by exercise.

If you exercise each day, you will also sleep better. An hour-long walk every day is ideal for most people, and if it is done with someone you like, it is also a great time to talk about the roller-coaster emotions you are now experiencing.

8. Get Rid Of Imagined Guilt

When a child or a spouse dies, sometimes those of us remaining experience guilt.

"I just saw her yesterday, and we ended up fighting. Oh, if we hadn't had that fight, she might not have gone out drinking and could have avoided the accident."

"If I would have said no when my son asked for the motorcycle, perhaps he would be alive today."

"If only I would have been a more loving wife, and given him everything that he wanted, maybe my husband would not have left me for that younger woman."

All of these types of statements are non-productive and only serve to evoke useless feelings of inadequacy.

If you have made mistakes in your relationships, that is all right; we all have. We all must learn to accept that we are imperfect. Only hindsight is 20/20.

If you are experiencing some severe guilt that is hampering your ability to live a productive life, consider professional counseling. Most Christian counselors are well-experienced in helping their clients work through the useless emotions and condemnation of guilt.

9. Accept Your Understanding Of The Loss

You have probably asked, "Why?" over and over in your mind, and perhaps you have even reached a small degree of understanding.

Just as time reduces the pain of a significant loss, it also increases your ability to understand the loss.

In time you will gain a greater perspective which leads to understanding and eventually acceptance
--life does go on.

10. Join A Group

Your old circle of friends may need to change. Even if it does not, you will need new friends for support. Bereaved people sometimes form groups for friendship, support, and sharing.

11. Associate With Old Friends

This may be difficult at first. Some of your friends may not be sure how to act around you. They want to help. They value your friendship but are not experienced in dealing with significant losses.

In time, they will learn how to interact with you if you give them a chance. You can help set the example by talking and acting as natural as possible and by not avoiding the subject of your loss.

12. Postpone Major Decisions!

This is one of the most vital guidelines I can give to you. Do not make any major decisions in your life for at least six months to a year.

No matter how deeply you "feel" about your current situation, make no major changes for at least six months.

13. Put Your Thoughts Into A Journal

If you are able to write, this process will help you get your feelings out and record your progress. Writing letters to say good-bye to your loved one can be painful, but the process is a helpful tool for many.

Writing is a worthwhile form of processing through your grief and should be seriously considered as a means of helping you release your hurts.

14. Turn Grief Into Creative Energy

Find a way to help others. Helping to carry someone else's load is guaranteed to lighten your own load, for example: Seek productive and creative activities that are centered on "others".

God has given each of us the ability to assist others, and when we do, we meet our own, God-given needs. The Apostle Paul understood this principle well when he, writing in his letter to the church in Corinth, related his desire and ability to comfort others in the areas he had received comfort from the Lord (II Corinthians 1:3-7).

15. If Necessary, Do Not Hesitate To Get Professional Help.

Because this is the last thing mentioned on my list, I do not intend for you to think this is the last thing you should try. If you find that your grief is crippling your ability to function for a long period of time, seek professional help.

It is important to remember that no matter how deep your sorrow, you are not alone! Others have been there and will help share your load if you will allow them.

You are loved; now let that love work for you in healing. Always remember, you are not alone. You have many friends, family, and Jesus Christ to minister to you and provide you with grief relief. Let them minister in love to your needs.

> *This time in your life will pass.*
> *You can and will make it through.*
> *Joy and hope will fill your life again.*
> *Let grief work its pain through.*
> *Remember, grief is the fruit of love.*

Everyone will experience loss in their own unique way. As a care-giver, you need to be just that -- a giver of care in the name of Jesus. All of us as members of the Body of Christ (the Church) are admonished to give care to others, as we pass through the valley. Let us remember the words of the Psalmist David.

PSALM 23

A Psalm of David

The LORD is my shepherd; I shall not want.

He makes me lie down in green pastures: he leads me beside the still waters.

He restores my soul: he leads me in the paths of righteousness for his name's sake.

Yes, though I walk through the valley of the shadow of death, I will fear no evil: for you are with me; your rod and your staff comfort me.

You prepare a table before me in the presence of my enemies: you anoint my head with oil; my cup runs over.

Surely goodness and mercy shall follow me all the days of my life: and I will dwell in the house of the LORD for ever.

Chapter Six:

Joy Comes in the Mourning

On January 24th 2000, my bride of 26 years, Karen, passed away. She had suffered under the ravages of brain cancer. My daughters, family and friends world wide suffered with us. Karen fought hard, she wanted to live, we went through the roller coaster of hope and despair, and on the morning of January 24th 2000 she died in faith.

My shock was profound, the sense of relief at the ending of Karen's suffering was overwhelming, but to my surprise, there was joy. Not joy in the death, for death from our view is an ugly thing. But after discovering that she was gone to be with the Father, an inner joy expressed in a spontaneous song rose up within me. I cannot remember nor explain the song but am grateful that the Holy Spirit provided such tangible comfort in the midst of my despair.

Later that evening, after robotically taking care of Karen's funeral arrangements and making numerous phone calls I attempted to sleep. It was fitful at best. Somewhere around two in the morning as I woke with a start, I heard from the Lord deep in my heart that he had a word for me and for the body of Christ. I was led to Hebrews 12:1-14. God spoke that in this passage I would find keys to finding the courage to survive a crisis of immense proportions. May it speak to you.

> *"Therefore, since we have so great a cloud of witnesses surrounding us, let us also lay aside every encumbrance and the sin which so easily entangles us, and let us run with endurance the race that is set before us, fixing our eyes on Jesus, the author and perfecter of faith, who for the joy set before Him endured the cross, despising the shame, and has sat down at the right hand of the throne of God.*
>
> *For consider Him who has endured such hostility by sinners against Himself, so that you will not grow weary and lose heart.*
>
> *You have not yet resisted to the point of shedding blood in your striving against sin; and you have forgotten the exhortation which is addressed to you as sons, 'My son, do not regard lightly the discipline of the lord, nor faint when you are reproved by him; for those whom the lord loves He disciplines, and He scourges every son whom He receives." It is for discipline that you endure; God deals with you as with sons; for what son is there whom his father does not discipline?*
>
> *But if you are without discipline, of which all have become partakers, then you are illegitimate children and not sons. Furthermore, we had*

earthly fathers to discipline us, and we respected them; shall we not much rather be subject to the Father of spirits, and live?

For they disciplined us for a short time as seemed best to them, but He disciplines us for our good, so that we may share His holiness.

All discipline for the moment seems not to be joyful, but sorrowful; yet to those who have been trained by it, afterwards it yields the peaceful fruit of righteousness. Therefore, strengthen the hands that are weak and the knees that are feeble, and make straight paths for your feet, so that the limb which is lame may not be put out of joint, but rather be healed.

Pursue peace with all men, and the sanctification without which no one will see the Lord. (NASB)

Here are the seven points God gave me when hope was gone, in the middle of shock and despair, at my lowest moment.

1. We all have a journey, a purpose to fulfill. Joseph had his purpose, but a pit, Potiphar's wife, prison and Pharaoh had to be faced and overcome before he saw the fulfillment of his purpose. Paul had a heavenly vision; Stephen saw heaven, and all died having fulfilled their purpose. Thus whether our journey is short or long, God is the Lord of the journey.

2. We are not alone in our journey. Even in our worst days, God will provide us with good comforters, friends to listen, and fellow travelers. We need them. We must journey with them.

3. We have a way maker, author and perfecter. Phil 1:6 became a personal promise and comfort for me in regard to Karen. It states, "I am confident in this very thing, that he who began a good work in you will perfect it until the day of Christ Jesus." Whatever the full purpose of Karen's life, I know she fulfilled it, because I know.

4. We... know struggles will come, pain and loss may (probably) be our experience but ultimately, as we trust in Christ there is joy. Karen's illness and death were hell for my family and me; we were not exempt; no one is. Why did Karen die...she contracted a deadly, incurable cancer. All of us will face crisis. We must trust God in spite of our circumstances, for we know he is faithful.

5. We... have a responsibility in our daily walk, which includes laying aside weights and sins, so we can complete our course. Grieving is necessary, mourning is healthy. None of us can carry the weight of grief alone, nor the sense of woundedness from our loss. Somehow with God's help we must lay it aside. Easier said than done,

but a necessary process. Further, we must recognize that, as unfair as it may seem, if we are still alive, we are to run our race, live our life for the long haul. Why Karen? Why not me?

6. All of us have normal questions, and rarely receive satisfactory answers. God is sovereign, but still we do not understand. Yet, if we keep our eyes on Jesus, we can find renewed purpose for our lives, especially as we consider all Christ has done for us.

7. We are to finish strong, which requires discipline. Discipline does not mean punishment. Though we might feel as though God is punishing us through our loss, this is certainly not true. God is love, and all circumstances we face will work out for good to those who love God and are called according to his purpose (Rom 8:28). Finishing strong, coming to acceptance, requires acknowledging our:

   a. Sonship... we are inheritors of the grace of God. We are part of God's family. That family has two locations -- here and in heaven. Karen will not come to me, but I will go to her in God's time. In the meantime, I must recognize my responsebility to act as a son (mature, equipped and prepared).

      b. Love from the Father…which is sure

      c. Submission to God's sovereignty, for God's ways are not ours, yet we know that "precious in the eyes of the Lord is the death of his saints (Psalm 116:15). I may never fully understand this yet I know I know.

8. We receive kingdom life, as we avoid a root of bitterness which can ruin us. We all have a choice, as we grieve, with God's help and much support to embrace God's Kingdom benefits, righteousness, peace and joy in the Holy Ghost (Rom 14:17) or we can reject God's love, grace, and mercy, to become bitter and refuse to grow.

A Wonderful Conclusion

Though we will all experience loss, we can endure, because the Holy Spirit lives within us. He is the Comforter, who in time will help us to know it <u>will</u> be well with our soul. Trust him, he is Good!

In the middle of my greatest loss, I sang a song, and danced a dance. He really does turn our mourning into dancing; by his grace, in time.

Books by the Author

- *A Christian Response to Crisis*
- *A Christian Response to Family Violence*
- *Addiction Counseling*
- *Crisis Counseling*
- *Family Violence: Patterns of Destruction*
- *Forty Days to the Promise: A Way Through the Wilderness*
- *From Hurt to Healed*
- *Grief Relief*
- *I Want to Be Like You, Dad*
- *Journey to Wholeness*
- *Marriage and Family Life: A Christian Perspective*
- *On Belay! Introduction to Christian Counseling*
- *Parenting on Purpose*
- *Patterns of Destruction*
- *The Bible in Counseling*
- *Group Dynamics* –DeKoven/Bohac
- *Human Development: A Christian Perspective*--DeKoven/Bohac

For a more in depth study on this topic, please refer to the book, "Grief Relief". This and all of Dr. Stan's books are available at www.booksbyvision.com

The Teaching Ministry of Dr. Stan DeKoven

Dr. Stan DeKoven conducts seminars and professional workshops, both nationally and internationally, based on his books and extensive experience in practical Christian living. He is available for limited engagements at church seminars, retreats and conferences. For a complete listing of topics and books, we invite you to contact:

Dr. Stan DeKoven, President
Vision International University and the International Training and Education Network
1672 Main Street E109
Ramona, CA. 92065
760-789-4700 (in California) or
1-800-9 VISION
Email: sdekoven@vision.edu
www.vision.edu

For your own copy of the handy reference sheet, or for more information on how Dr. Stan can offer you individualized coaching or other assistance, please visit his website at www.drstandekoven.com

www.ingramcontent.com/pod-product-compliance
Lightning Source LLC
Chambersburg PA
CBHW061513040426
42450CB00008B/1590